629.4

**Books are to be returned on or before
the last date below.**

LIBREX —

SPACE EXPLORATION

BRIAN JONES

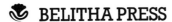 BELITHA PRESS

First published in Great Britain in 1990 by
Belitha Press Limited
31 Newington Green, London N16 9PU
Copyright © Belitha Press Limited and
Gareth Stevens, Inc. 1990
Illustrations/photographs copyright © in this
format by Belitha Press Limited and Gareth
Stevens, Inc. 1990
ISBN 1 85561 008 6
Typeset by Chambers Wallace, London
Printed in the UK for Imago Publishing
by MacLehose and Partners

British Library Cataloguing in Publication Data
CIP data for this book is available from the British
Library

Acknowledgements

Photographic credits:

Bernard Abrams 29 bottom
Chris Floyd 31
Robert Harding Picture Library 5, 6, 22, 29 top, 32
    bottom
NASA 14/15, 17, 20, 21, 25, 32/33, 40 left, 47, 48, 49,
    52 left, 54
Copyright National Geographic Society, paintings
    by Jean-Leon Huens 8, 9 bottom, 11, 34 bottom
Novosti 46
Ronan Picture Library 9 top
Royal Aeronautical Society 7
Science Photo Library 10, 15, 23, 30, 40 right, 44, 48,
    49, 53, 58 left
Chris Walker 27 top

Illustrated by: Julian Baum, Angus McKie (Young
Artists) and Eugene Fleury

Series editor: Neil Champion
Educational consultant: Dr Alistair Ross
Editorial consultant: Neil Morris
Designed by: Groom and Pickerill
Picture research and art editing: Ann Usborne
Specialist consultant: Martin Wace

Contents

Words found in **bold** are explained
in the glossary on pages 60 and 61

1: LOOKING AT SPACE

Our Place in the Universe

The Earth in Space

The planet Earth was once thought to be the most important place in the universe. However, the Earth is quite insignificant. It is special to human beings only because it is home. It moves on its path about the Sun along with the other **planets** of the **solar system**. The Sun appears large and bright because it is close to us. In reality it is just an ordinary **star**, one of many billions of stars within the **Galaxy**. The Galaxy is one of a cluster of galaxies. Other, similar clusters are seen scattered

This is our Solar System as we know it today. The Sun is at the centre, with the planets going round it. These planets are: Mercury, Venus, Earth, Mars, Jupiter, Saturn, Uranus, Neptune and Pluto. They move in oval-shaped (elliptical) orbits. They vary in size, from Mercury (the smallest, at 4,880 km in diameter) to Jupiter (the largest, at 142,800 km in diameter). ▶

Light Years

The distances between Earth and the stars are very great. **Astronomers** do not use miles or kilometres to measure how far away they are. They use a unit of length called a **light year**. This is the distance that a ray of light would travel in one year. Light travels very quickly, at 300,000 km (186,000 miles) every second. A light year is equal to almost 10 million million kilometres.

Our Solar System

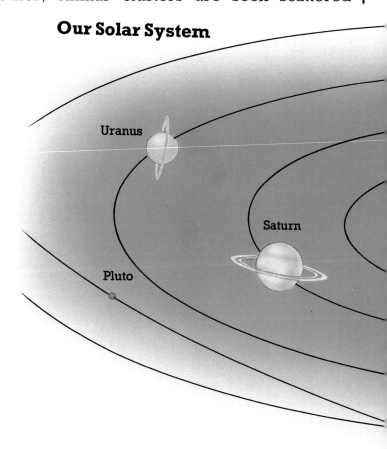

Uranus

Saturn

Pluto

throughout the universe. Many of these are much bigger than ours.

Studying the Stars

Astronomers use **telescopes** to look at the night sky. These help them to study light given out by the stars. Stars and other objects in space also give off something called **radio waves**. These radio waves cannot be seen. Special **radio telescopes** help us to study these radio waves. There are lots of other forms of energy coming from the sky. Astronomers have built special instruments and telescopes which can pick these up. By using these we can learn much more about the stars.

The universe is a wonderful place and contains many strange, beautiful and exciting objects. Anyone can take an interest in the night sky, and you don't need a telescope to do so. In this book we will take a closer look at the stars. Exploring space may even lead to people **colonizing** other planets.

▲ The 70 metre diameter radio telescope at Jodrell Bank, England is one of the largest telescopes of its kind in the world. It is specially designed to detect radio waves from the stars and other objects in the sky.

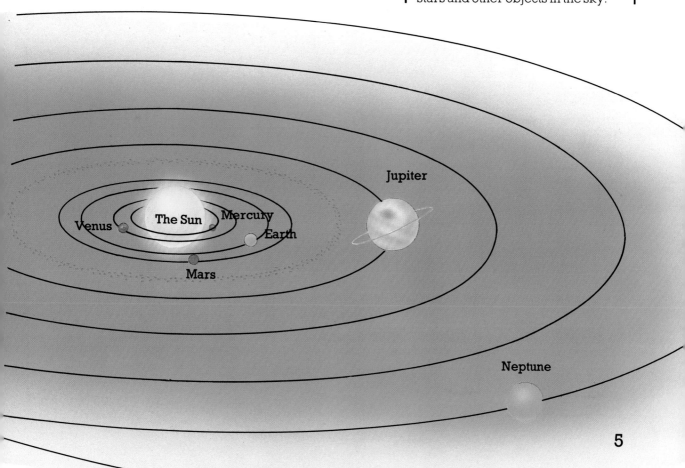

Jupiter

Venus   The Sun   Mercury
                              Earth

Mars

Neptune

5

The First Star-Gazers

The River Nile in Egypt floods at the same time every year. Ancient Egyptians could tell when this would happen by watching the stars. A star called Sirius would appear in the dawn sky every year just before the flooding would start. ▼

For thousands of years people believed that the Earth was at the centre of the Universe. They thought that the Sun, Moon, planets and stars moved in a circle around it. It was also generally believed that the Earth was flat. If you sailed to the horizon you would fall off the edge! Today we know both these things to be wrong. The **telescope** has helped us to find this out. But the first astronomers did not have the help of this invention. They had only eyes and their imaginations.

The Ancient Greeks (700BC-AD100)

Some of the Greek astronomers questioned whether the Earth was really flat. Aristotle used mathematics and the simple observation that the horizon changed depending on where you were standing, to work out that the Earth was really round. Another Greek worked out that the Earth really travelled around the Sun. Both these ideas were not very popular at the time. Not many people listened to them.

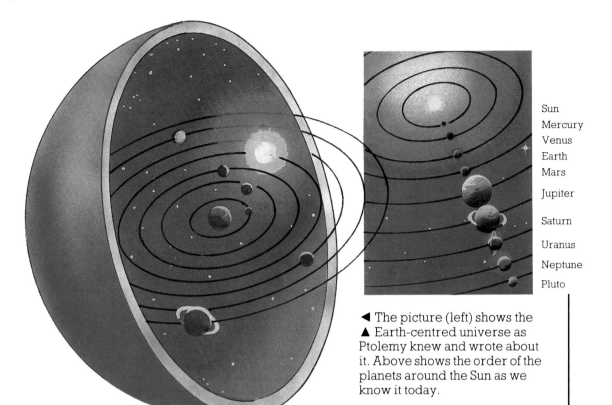

Sun
Mercury
Venus
Earth
Mars

Jupiter

Saturn

Uranus

Neptune

Pluto

◀ The picture (left) shows the
▲ Earth-centred universe as
Ptolemy knew and wrote about
it. Above shows the order of the
planets around the Sun as we
know it today.

What people did believe was summed up by
the last Greek astronomer. His name was
Ptolemy. He wrote a book in which he put
down all the ideas about the Earth-centred
Universe. This model became known as the
Ptolemaic Universe. He died in AD180 and with
him died Greek interest in studying the planets
and stars.

Arabic Astronomy

A few hundred years after Ptolemy, the Arabs
revived interest in studying the heavens. They
drew very accurate star charts. Their sailors
used them for navigation. The Greeks had also
used their knowledge of star patterns to find
their way around by night at sea.

In spite of the accuracy of their recordings,
progress in astronomy was slow. This was
mainly due to their belief that the Earth was at
the centre of everything. This belief was not
seriously challenged until a Polish astronomer
in 1546 put forward the view that the Sun was
the centre of the universe. His name was
Nicolas Copernicus.

This is a Chinese star map. It
shows the position of the stars
in the sky. ▼

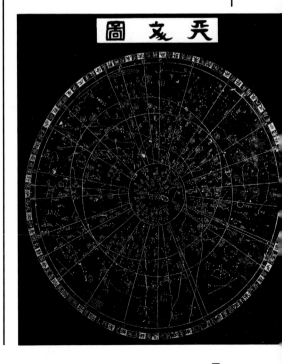

Changing Ideas

Nicolaus Copernicus

Nicolaus Copernicus was born in 1473 and during his lifetime he studied the movement of the planets through the sky. As he made his observations, he realized that Ptolemy's Theory could not explain the way the planets moved. He suggested that the Sun, not the Earth, was at the centre of the universe. All the planets, including the Earth, travelled around the Sun in **orbits** that Copernicus thought were circular. He wrote a book explaining his ideas but this was dangerous. The Catholic Church thought that the Earth, as the most important planet in the universe, was at the centre. To argue against this teaching led to punishment. Copernicus knew this, and did not publish his book until 1543, the year in which he died. Even his Theory did not offer a complete explanation for the way the planets move.

The Work of Tycho Brahe

Tycho Brahe (1546-1601) was a Danish astronomer. From his **observatory** at Hveen, off the Swedish coast, he made many accurate observations of the stars and planets. Brahe was a keen observer and the star charts he drew up were more accurate than any made before.

Johannes Kepler

When Brahe died in 1601, his assistant, Johannes Kepler took over his work. Kepler knew that Brahe's observations of the planets were very accurate. However, their movements through the sky did not quite fit in with the circular orbits suggested by Copernicus. He realized where Copernicus had gone wrong. The planets did go round the Sun, but their orbits were not circular. They were **elliptical** – their distances from the Sun varied. He also discovered that a planet travelled faster when it was closest to the Sun.

Johannes Kepler was a brilliant mathematician. His work had finally shown how the planets moved around a central Sun, which the Church eventually accepted.

▲ Nicolaus Copernicus, the Polish astronomer, who wrote a book in which he suggested that the planets orbited the Sun. He is seen here in his study with an open copy of Ptolemy's book.

Tycho Brahe's Observatory

◀ Tycho Brahe was an excellent observer who made very accurate measurements of star positions and movements of the planets. This is his observatory on the island of Hveen, off the Swedish coast.

◀ Johannes Kepler used Tycho Brahe's observations to discover that the planets do not move in a circle around the Sun. Using mathematics, he explained the laws of planetary motion, showing the elliptical nature of a planet's orbit around the Sun.

Elliptical path a planet takes around the Sun

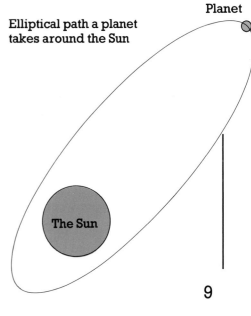

Planet

The Sun

Telescopes

Kitt Peak National Observatory, Arizona, USA. The large observatory building at the centre contains the 4-metre (158-inch) Mayall Telescope, one of the world's largest telescopes. ▶

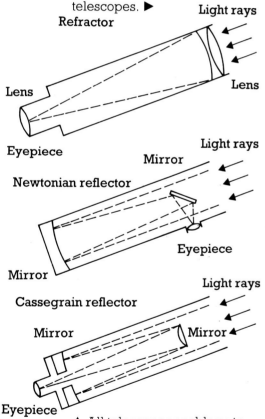

Refractor

Light rays

Lens

Lens

Eyepiece

Newtonian reflector

Light rays

Mirror

Mirror

Eyepiece

Cassegrain reflector

Light rays

Mirror

Mirror

Eyepiece

▲ All telescopes enable us to see things that are far away, much more clearly. They do this by making the image bigger. Early telescopes were refractors which used a lens to collect starlight. Reflectors use mirrors instead of a lens.

Early Telescopes

The telescope was used in 1609 for the first time to study the stars. The Italian astronomer Galileo Galilei used the telescope to make many important discoveries, including seeing for the first time the four largest moons of Jupiter and the different **phases** of Venus. He also saw the **Milky Way** was made up of the combined light of many thousands of distant stars. His observations convinced him that the Earth and other planets went round the Sun. Galileo made his own telescopes. The most powerful had a **magnification** of 30 times. They were the **refracting** type, which means that they used a lens to collect starlight.

Knowledge of the universe grew as telescopes improved. A new type of telescope was invented. This was the **reflector**, which uses a mirror, and not a lens, to collect light. The first was made by Isaac Newton in 1668.

Astronomical Observatories

Today, large telescopes are kept in special buildings called observatories. These are found the world over, especially in the USA. One famous example is the Kitt Peak National Observatory. This is near Tucson in Arizona. There are many different telescopes here. Astronomers who visit Kitt Peak come from all over the world. They can live there for a long time, studying the stars. Similar to this is the Cerro Tololo Inter-American Observatory, situated high on a mountain in Chile, South America.

European astronomers carry out observations from La Palma, one of the Canary Islands. The observatory is situated 2,400 m (7,870 ft) above sea-level on an extinct volcano. From here, astronomers take advantage of the dark, clear skies that are essential when observing the night sky.

▲ William Herschel (1738-1822) was an amateur astronomer. He discovered the planet Uranus on 13th March 1781, using a telescope he had built. For many years he held the record for the largest telescope in the world.

Did You Know?

Larger telescopes were made. The size of a telescope is shown by the **diameter** of its main lens or mirror. The largest for many years was a 120 cm (48 inch) reflector telescope made by William Herschel in 1789.

11

2: INTO SPACE

The Earth in Space

A photograph of Earth taken by Apollo astronauts returning from the Moon. North and South America can be clearly seen with the Pacific and Atlantic Oceans on either side. ▶

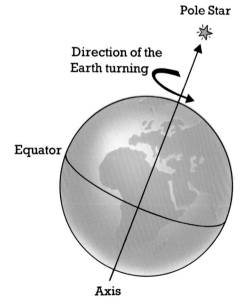

Pole Star

Direction of the Earth turning

Equator

Axis

▲ The Earth spins on its axis, taking 24 hours to complete one revolution.

The Earth travels around the Sun in an orbit which takes $365\frac{1}{4}$ days to complete. Our calendar year has 365 days. This means that there is a quarter of a day left over each year. This is used every four years to make an extra day. The year with the extra day is called a leap year and has 366 days. February has 29 days instead of the usual 28. This addition of an extra day every four years brings the calendar back in line.

The Seasons

As Kepler discovered, the Earth's orbit is not circular. In December it is slightly closer to the Sun than in June, when it is at its farthest point away. Earth is also tilted on an **axis**. In June, the northern hemisphere is tilted *towards* the Sun. It is then summer in the northern hemisphere and winter in the southern hemisphere. In December it is tilted *away* from the Sun, making it winter in the north and summer in the south.

In March and September neither hemisphere is tilted towards the Sun. The days and nights are of equal length. In March the northern hemisphere has its spring and the southern hemisphere its autumn. In September the situation is the other way round.

Other planets have their own seasons and orbital periods. The length of a planet's year is the time it takes to go once around the Sun. If you lived on Mercury, your year would be only 88 Earth-days. On Pluto, the outermost known planet, the year is equal to 248 years on Earth!

Earth Facts

- The Earth is about 4,700 million years old.

- The Earth is not a perfect round shape. Its circumference at the equator is 40,077 km (24,903 miles), and at the Poles it is 40,009 km (24,861 miles).

- The Earth has two hemispheres: the northern hemisphere and the southern hemisphere. They are separated by the equator.

- The Earth is about 150 million km (93 million miles) from the Sun.

This diagram shows how in moving around the Sun in an elliptical path, the seasons occur. At different times of the year, the Earth is further away from the Sun. Also, because it is tilted on an axis, parts of the Earth point towards or away from the Sun. ▼

The Seasons

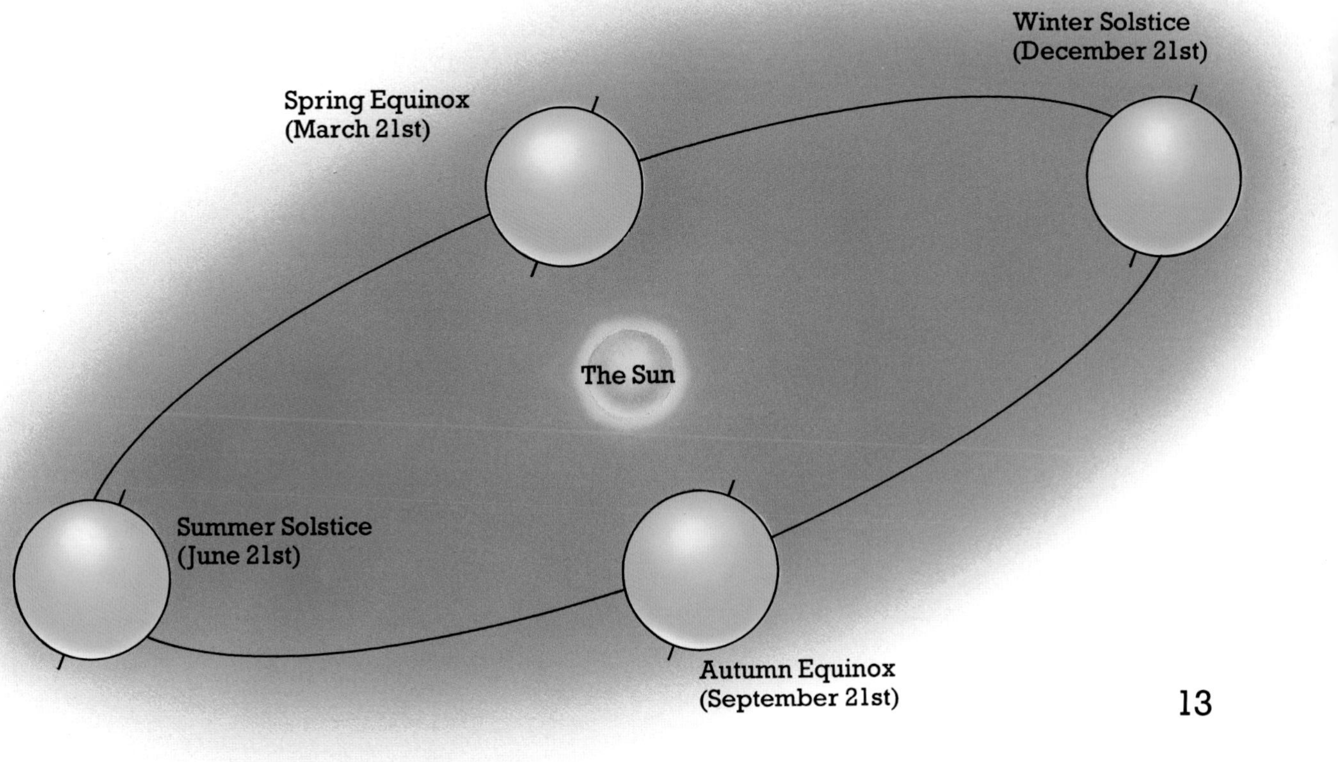

Winter Solstice (December 21st)

Spring Equinox (March 21st)

The Sun

Summer Solstice (June 21st)

Autumn Equinox (September 21st)

13

The Sun

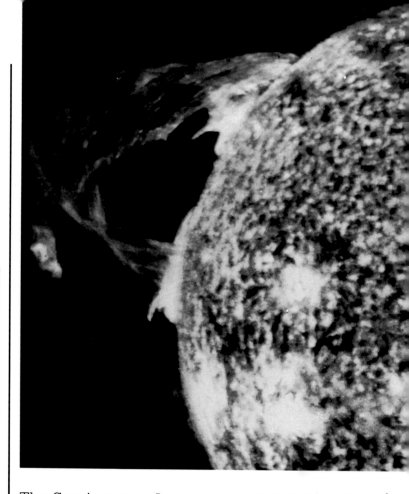

Did You Know?

The Sun was formed a very long time ago inside a cloud of gas and dust. There are clouds like this all over the Galaxy, called nebulae (see pages 30-31). The Sun and its planets were made from a nebula.

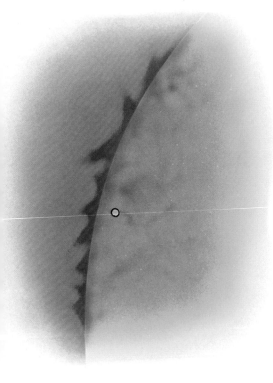

▲ The Sun is huge. It is 100 times greater in diameter than the Earth. It is also extremely hot. In its centre the temperature is around 15 million degrees Celsius.

The Sun is a star. It seems much brighter than all the other stars because it is much closer to Earth. Many of the other stars are actually hotter and brighter. The Sun gives out energy in the forms of light and heat. Without this energy there would be no life on Earth. The Sun also lights up the Moon, the planets and their satellites, comets and everything else in the Solar System. These objects only shine because they are reflecting light from the Sun. If the Sun were to go out suddenly, then all these objects would seem to disappear.

How the Sun Produces Energy

The Sun is not really burning. It is producing heat and light energy by changing one kind of **gas** into another. It does this in a special way. Two **atoms** of **hydrogen** are forced together to make **helium**. When this happens, there is a tiny bit of material left over. This makes its way to the surface of the Sun where it escapes as light and heat. The Sun loses a lot of weight this

14

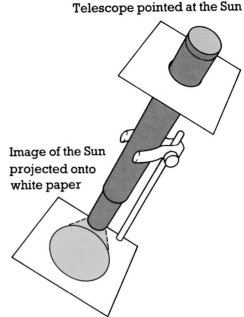

Telescope pointed at the Sun

Image of the Sun projected onto white paper

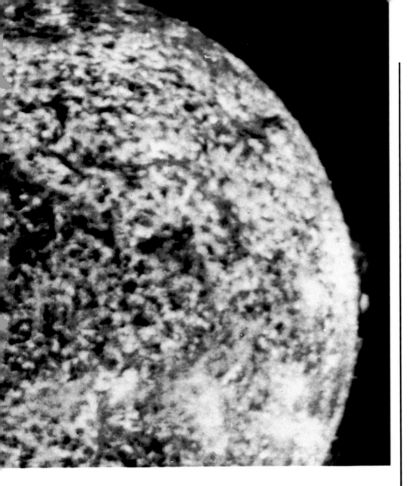

way but it is so large that it will last for a very long time yet.

Sunspots and Prominences

The Sun sometimes has dark patches on its surface. These are sunspots and they appear dark because they are cooler than the surrounding area. Sunspots mainly appear in groups and can last anything from a few hours to a few months, depending on their size. Large sunspots last longer. If a sunspot is watched for a few days, it will be seen to cross the face of the Sun. This is because the Sun is turning on its axis. The Sun takes about a month to make one complete turn.

Clouds of hot gas can often be seen above the surface of the Sun. These are called **prominences**. Normally, special equipment is needed to catch sight of them. This is because they are lost in the glare of the sun. However, they can be seen during a total solar eclipse (see pages 24-25).

◀ A huge **prominence** can be seen coming from the Sun's surface.

Sunspots ▼

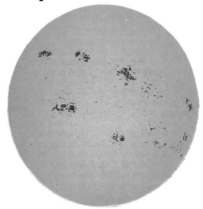

Beware!

You must NEVER look at the Sun directly, either with the naked eye or through binoculars or a telescope. The Sun is very bright and will certainly damage your eyes. You may even be permanently blinded. The only safe way to observe the Sun is by projecting its image onto a piece of white card or something similar. This can be done either with binoculars or a telescope as shown in the diagram.

The Moon

This diagram shows the phases of the Moon. This starts with the new, leading to the full and ending with the old Moon. It takes 29½ days for this cycle to come back to the beginning. The Moon appears to change shape because at different phases some of its surface may be hidden to viewers on Earth. ▶

The Moon has about one sixth the pull of gravity compared with that on Earth. This is why people can jump higher and hit things further on the Moon. ▶

Moon Facts

● The Moon is about 380,000 km (238,000 miles) away from the Earth. It is our closest neighbour in space.

● The Moon revolves around the earth. It takes 27¼ days to do this.

● The diameter of the Moon is 3,476 km (2,159 miles). It is quite a small satellite. Nevertheless, its gravitational pull causes the seas and oceans on Earth to move in and out. We call these movements, tides.

Earth's Satellite

The Moon is the closest neighbour in space to Earth and astronomers have studied it for centuries mainly through telescopes. More recently, **space probes** have sent back pictures and information from the Moon itself. People have even landed on the Moon and carried out experiments on its surface. Because of all this, we now know a great deal about this natural **satellite**.

Astronomers believe that the Moon formed separately from the Earth. It was then captured by the Earth's **gravity** and has been going round our planet ever since. The Moon has no **atmosphere** and from its surface the sky appears black. It is very hot during the **lunar** day and very cold during the night.

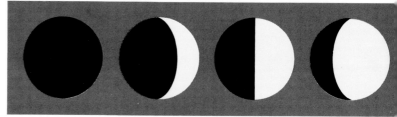

The Surface of the Moon

The Moon is covered with light and dark areas. The light areas are covered with craters formed when meteorites hit the surface. Some of these craters have diameters up to 160 km (100 miles) or more. The dark areas are vast, flat plains. These were formed by **lava** from volcanoes which spilled out on to the Moon's surface. These dark areas are known as 'maria' or 'seas' because the astronomers used to think that these regions were like the Earth's oceans and seas. We now know that there is no water on the Moon, but the names given to these areas are still used. One of the most famous is the Sea of Tranquillity. It was here in 1969 that people first set foot on the Moon, during the USA Apollo 11 mission.

▲ Astronauts on board the Apollo 10 craft took this photograph of the far side of the Moon. It shows a very rugged area with lots of craters.

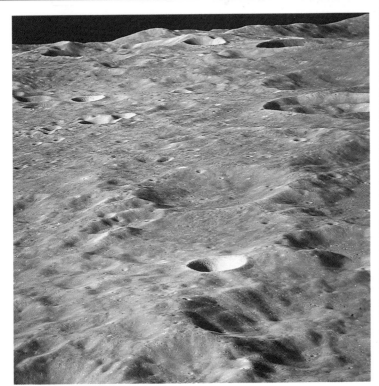

◄ The surface of the Moon.

This diagram shows that in orbit around the Earth, the Moon keeps the same face turned towards us. ▼

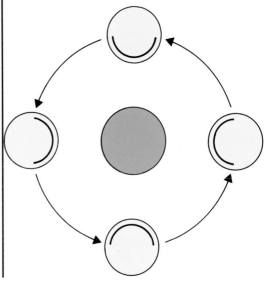

3: THE SOLAR SYSTEM

The Inner Planets

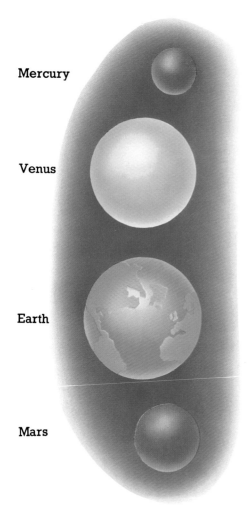

Mercury

Venus

Earth

Mars

▲ These are the four inner planets: Mercury, Venus, the Earth and Mars.

Venus lies closer to the Sun than Earth. Like the Moon, it has phases when we can see more or less of it. ▶

The planets in the Solar System are split into two groups. There are four small inner plants and four outer planets which are much larger and made up mainly of gas. In between these two groups are the minor planets (see pages 22-23). The outermost planet is Pluto. It is so far away that astronomers know little about it.

Mercury

The closest planet to the Sun is Mercury. It is difficult to see from Earth because it always appears very close to the Sun. It can be seen either low in the east before sunrise or low in the west after sunset. It wasn't until an unmanned spacecraft flew past the planet and sent back photographs that we saw what Mercury was really like. It has a large number of craters. There are some mountains and one or two flat areas like those on the Moon. Mercury is very hot and has no atmosphere or water. There is no life on Mercury.

Venus

The next planet out from the Sun is Venus. This is the brightest object in the sky apart from the Sun and Moon. Although Venus appears beautiful when seen in the sky, it is a very hostile planet. It is covered in clouds of poisonous gases which reflect sunlight very well. The

The Phases of Venus

These outer circles show how much of Venus we can see from Earth.

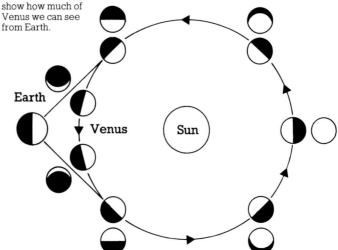

Earth

Venus

Sun

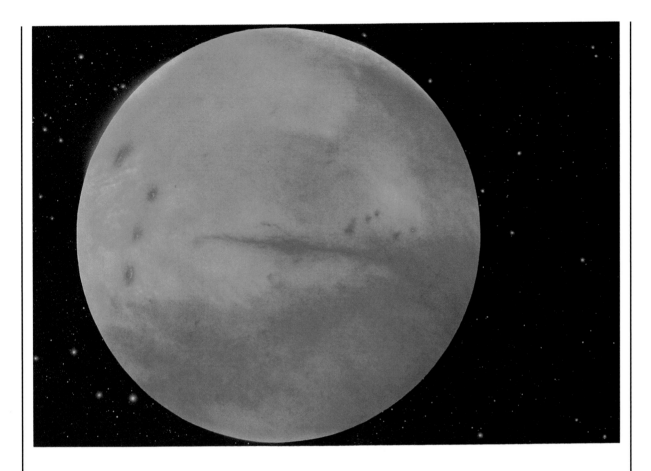

surface is extremely hot and the clouds are so thick that the Sun cannot be seen through them. Recent unmanned space missions to the planet have used special instruments to map its surface. Venus has many large flat plains together with craters, valleys and mountainous regions. There are also volcanoes which may still be active.

Mars

Mars appears as a red, starlike point when seen in the sky. The ancient astronomers named it after the god of war because it was the same colour as blood.

When seen through a telescope, Mars reveals its polar ice caps which contain frozen water. Years ago, astronomers thought that Mars may contain intelligent life. We now know that this is not true. Many unmanned spacecraft have visited the planet and sent back photographs. Two have even landed there (see Probes to the Planets) and looked for signs of life, although they didn't find any. However, they did show us that the surface of Mars is very cold and covered with rocks of all sizes.

Mars has many different surface features. There are many craters, mountains and valleys and

▲ This is a view of Mars, the red planet.

lofty volcanoes. One of these volcanoes is the largest in the Solar System. It is called Olympus Mons and is over 25 kms (15 miles) high. It is over 700 kms (430 miles) in diameter.

Mars has two moons, although both are very small and only a few miles across. They are called Phobos and Deimos and large telescopes are needed to see them. It may be that they are actually minor planets that wandered so close to Mars that they ended up in orbit around it.

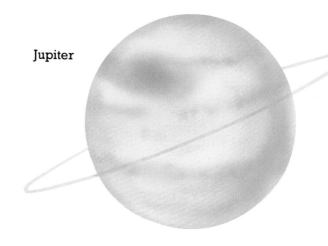

Jupiter

The Outer Planets

Saturn

Pluto

Neptune

Uranus

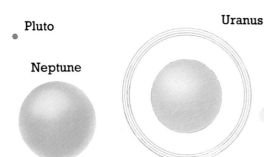

▲ These are the five outer planets: Jupiter, Saturn, Uranus, Neptune and Pluto.

This is a photograph of Jupiter, taken from Voyager 1. You can see the Great Red Spot, which is thought to be a gigantic storm. ▼

Jupiter

Beyond the region of the minor planets is Jupiter, the largest planet in the Solar System. Like the other gaseous planets, Jupiter does not have a solid surface. When Jupiter is looked at through even a small telescope cloud belts can be seen crossing the planet. There is also the famous Great Red Spot which is thought to be a gigantic storm taking place in Jupiter's atmosphere. Jupiter has a very short day, taking less than ten hours to spin once on its axis.

There are a total of sixteen moons in orbit around Jupiter. The four largest of these can be seen through binoculars or a small telescope. One of these is Io, which has a large number of active volcanoes on its surface. Callisto, another of the satellites, has a surface which is almost completely covered in craters.

Saturn

Saturn is the second largest planet in the Solar System. Cloud belts can be seen crossing Saturn, although these are not as easy to see as those of Jupiter. There are at least 21 moons going around it. The largest of these is Titan which is a lot bigger than Earth's Moon.

The rings around Saturn make it one of the most beautiful sights in the sky. These rings can be seen

Pluto   Neptune   Uranus   Saturn   Jupiter   Earth   Sun

through a small telescope. They are made up of millions of tiny icy particles.

Uranus

Uranus also has rings but they are very faint and difficult to see from Earth. There are also fifteen moons moving around the planet. Only the five largest of these can be seen from Earth. The rest were discovered by the Voyager 2 spacecraft in 1986.

Uranus has a very long "year" and takes 84 Earth-years to travel once around the Sun. It also has a very large axial tilt. This means that it orbits the Sun on its side and that the poles and the equator take turns to face the Sun!

Therefore there are times when the polar regions of Uranus are warmer than the equator.

Neptune

Neptune is the most distant of the gas planets. It orbits the Sun over a billion miles further away than Uranus, taking 165 years to do so. So far we know Neptune has two moons. The Voyager 2 spacecraft passing the planet in 1989 will send back to Earth more information about it.

Pluto

The outermost planet is Pluto. This is a small and very faint world and we know little about it. Pluto

▲ These lines show part of the orbits around the Sun of the five outer planets.

has one moon called Charon, which is half as big as Pluto itself. At the moment there are no planned space missions to Pluto. So it might be a long time yet before we learn more about this planet.

If there are any more planets beyond Pluto they will be very faint and difficult to detect. However, some astronomers think that there may be other planets to find.

This is a photograph of Saturn taken from Voyager 2. You can see the Moons, Rhea and Dione, as blue dots to the south and southeast. ▼

Comets

Comets are made up of water, ice and dust. They are very small and cannot be seen when they are a long way from the Sun. As a comet nears the Sun it is warmed up. As the ice melts the dust and gases escape, forming a cloud, or coma, around the comet. Eventually, this gas and dust is blown away from the coma by the Sun's energy. It forms one or more tails which stretch away from the head of the comet. However, not all comets have tails. Some have made so many close approaches to the Sun that the energy from our star has caused them to lose most of their material. When this happens, there isn't enough dust and gas left to form a tail. These comets become very faint and appear only as fuzzy patches of light.

Halley's Comet is the most famous of all the comets and was first recorded over 2,000 years ago. It orbits the Sun every 76 years. This picture was taken in March 1986 during its last visit to the inner Solar System. ▶

The Asteroid Belt

Minor Planets

These are tiny planetary bodies, also called **asteroids**, most of which orbit the Sun between the paths of Mars and Jupiter. Some minor planets move well away from this region. Hidalgo travels out beyond Saturn and the asteroid Icarus moves closer to the Sun than Mercury. The minor planets are all very faint and only one, Vesta, can be seen without a telescope or binoculars. It is thought that the minor planets are material left over from when the Solar System was formed.

The Asteroid Belt

Meteors and Meteorites

As a comet goes around the Sun it leaves dust behind which spreads out along its path. If any of this dust comes close to Earth it can be pulled down by the Earth's gravity. It enters the atmosphere at very high speeds and burns up. The result is a **meteor** which we see as a streak of light. Meteors are often called *shooting stars,* although they have nothing to all to do with stars.

Some parts are large enough to survive the fall through the atmosphere and land on the surface of our planet. These are **meteorites**, and when they land they can produce craters, rather like those of the Moon. Many meteorite craters have been found. Meteorites are fairly common but we do not know of anyone being killed by one. However, if a large meteorite ever fell on a city or town, a great deal of damage could be caused.

▲ The Arizona Meteorite Crater was formed by a meteorite that fell thousands of years ago.

As a particle enters the atmosphere it burns up. ▼

Eclipses

Eclipses of the Moon

The only reason that we see the Moon is because it reflects light from the Sun. A lunar eclipse takes place when the Moon passes into the Earth's shadow. During a lunar eclipse, the Moon's surface becomes quite dark. Lunar eclipses occur more often than solar eclipses. During a lunar eclipse, the Moon does not usually disappear completely. This is because the Earth's atmosphere bends sunlight on to the Moon's surface. However, the Moon can sometimes disappear completely. This does not happen very often. The earliest record of this happening was in AD 753.

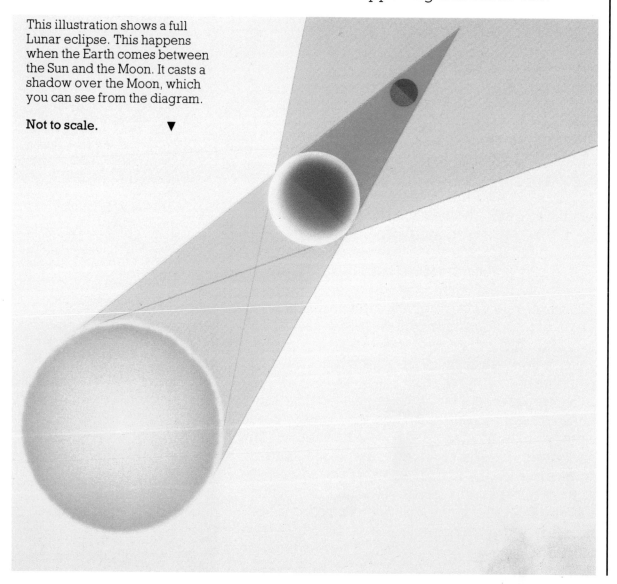

This illustration shows a full Lunar eclipse. This happens when the Earth comes between the Sun and the Moon. It casts a shadow over the Moon, which you can see from the diagram.

Not to scale. ▼

Eclipses of the Sun

Although the Sun is a lot bigger than the Moon, it is also a lot further away. That is why both look the same size in the sky. The new Moon is positioned between the Sun and the Earth. Its dark side is facing us and we cannot see it. At most new Moon phases, the Moon passes either just above or just below the Sun as seen from the Earth. However, if the Moon passes exactly between the Sun and the Earth we see a solar eclipse.

Because the Moon travels around the Earth once a month, you may think that a solar eclipse should occur every time. The reason that the Sun, Moon and Earth are not exactly in line each time there is a new Moon is easy to understand. The path of the Moon is tilted. This means that the Moon misses the Sun almost every time.

Total eclipses of the Sun occur when the Moon comes between the Sun and Earth and completely hides it. When this happens, the sky becomes quite dark and stars can be seen. The last total solar eclipse visible from Britain was in 1927 and the next will be in 1999. Eclipses can be seen from many places on the Earth. Not all are total eclipses. Sometimes only part of the Sun is hidden by the Moon.

The photograph (left) shows special radar equipment that is used in monitoring Solar eclipses. The photograph (above) shows a Solar eclipse happening. This occurs when the moon comes between the Earth and Sun.

Did You Know?

Many people have seen eclipses as being magical or an omen. Some made stories up to explain what was happening. In China, it was thought that a dragon was eating the Sun. Gongs and drums were beaten to frighten the dragon away. In 585 BC, two armies who were fighting each other were so awed by a total eclipse that they made peace!

4: THE UNIVERSE BEYOND

The Stars

Constellations

At first sight, the night sky appears to be a jumbled mass of stars. From earliest times people have looked at those stars and found patterns or **constellations**. Although stars are moving through space, they all lie at very great distances from each other and so their positions hardly appear to alter, even over many centuries. It is the same effect as watching a bird fly nearby and a jet flying many miles away. Although the jet appears to be moving much slower than the bird, this is only because it is so much further away.

The stars in a constellation are not really close together. They all lie at different distances and only appear close to each other because they are situated in roughly the same direction as seen from Earth.

There are a total of 88 constellations. Some of these, like Orion (the Hunter) and Ursa Major (the Great Bear), are easy to locate. However, there are some which are small and faint.

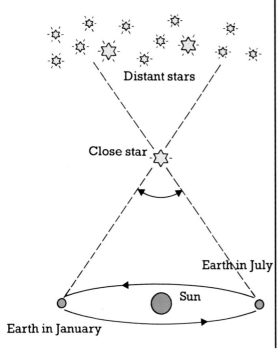

▲ These diagrams (above and right) show how by using an object relatively close at hand, you can measure the distances of objects further away. To do this, you need to compare the angle from two different places. ▶

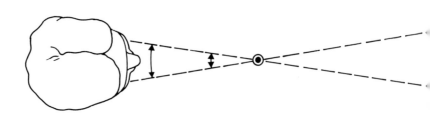

Distances of the Stars

The first star to have its distance measured can be found in the constellation of Cygnus, the Swan. This was worked out by the German astronomer Friedrich Bessel in 1838. He found that the star was about 11 light years away.

For very distant stars, astronomers use a different method to work out their distances. They find out the star's true brightness, and then compare it with a closer star of known distance and with a similar true brightness. This is like looking at two candles, one of which is quite close and the other a long way off. If you know that they are really as bright as each other, you can work out how far away the more distant one is by comparing them. Each star in the sky has its own colour. Some of the brighter ones, such as the orange-red Betelgeuse in the constellation of Orion and the brilliant white Sirius, have colours that can be easily seen with the naked eye. The colour of a star tells us a lot about it, including its temperature, age and general condition. This in turn helps astronomers to work out the actual brightness.

Star Brightness

The stars all appear to have different brightnesses. The brightness of a star (or other object in the sky, such as a planet) is known as its **magnitude**. The lower the number the brighter the star. The faintest stars visible to the naked eye are magnitude 6, while very bright stars are magnitude 0, or zero. Some stars are so bright they they have a minus number. The star Sirius in the constellation of Canis Major, the Great Dog, has a magnitude of minus 1.4, and is the brightest star in the sky apart from the Sun.

These values indicate how bright a star appears to us here on Earth. In reality, a star of magnitude 6 may be much brighter than one of magnitude 0, and may only seem much fainter because it is so much further away.

The Life of a Star

Stars are made inside giant clouds of gas and dust. Parts of the cloud collect together to form the star, which at first is cool. The star shrinks under the pull of gravity and warms up. The centre becomes so hot that the star begins to produce light and heat in the same way as our Sun (see pages 14-15).

When the star's fuel is used up, the star changes. The star becomes a **red giant**. This will happen to the Earth's Sun – but a very long time from now. Eventually, stars like the Sun lose their outer layers while the inner regions collapse to form a **white dwarf**. These are very dense and heavy: a cupful of white dwarf material may weigh many tons! White dwarfs shine faintly and cannot be seen without the help of a telescope. Eventually they stop shining, leaving a cold, dark globe.

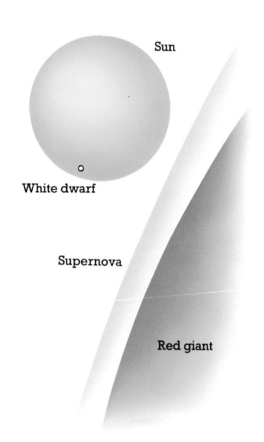

Sun

White dwarf

Supernova

Red giant

▲ In these diagrams you can see the evolutionary stages of a Star's life. These include the red giant and white dwarf stages. ▶

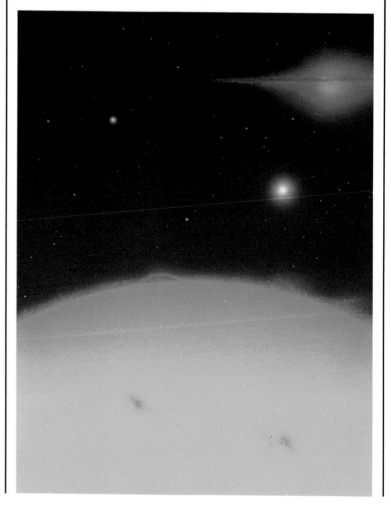

Some stars use up their fuel at a quicker rate and then explode, sending most of their material into space. This explosion is called a **supernova**. Clouds of material are left which spread out into surrounding space. The central regions of these stars collapse and form objects that are much heavier than white dwarfs. Just a spoonful of this material would weigh millions of tons.

Double Stars

Sometimes, what looks to us like a single Sun is really a pair of stars in orbit around each other. These are known as binary systems.

Variable Stars

Many stars shine steadily, although there are some whose brightness changes over periods ranging from a few hours to many weeks. These variable stars are of different kinds, including those that actually swell and contract, getting brighter and dimmer.

▲ This is a supernova remnant – the clouds of material left in space after a star has exploded.

The double star, Albireo, in the constellation Cygnus. ▼

Nebulae and Star Clusters

Nebulae

Nebulae are clouds of gas and dust and can be seen scattered throughout space. Many of them are bright, because they are lit up by stars inside them. Other nebulae are dark. There are no stars inside them and they appear as dark patches against the starry background.

Many bright nebulae are visible through binoculars or small telescopes, and a few can be seen with the unaided eye. One of these is the Orion Nebula, a faint patch of light (when looked at without a telescope or binoculars). Dark nebulae are very difficult to see. If you want to look at dark nebulae you will need a large telescope.

Star Clusters

The gas inside the Orion Nebula is collecting together to form stars. Eventually the cloud will collapse to form a star cluster. Stars are being born inside other nebulae all the time. These are known as open clusters. There are two types of star cluster: open and globular.

▲ The Orion Nebula is easily visible to the naked eye.

The Pleiades is a young open star cluster originally formed from a nebula. ▶

Open Clusters

These are also called galactic clusters. This is because they are found along the main plane of our Milky Way Galaxy (see pages 32-33). Open clusters are loose collections of stars with no definite shape. We can see lots of these in the sky. Two that are easy to find are the Hyades and the Pleiades (see page 39). The Pleiades are young stars and some of the gas from the original nebula can still be seen surrounding them. The Hyades are a much older cluster. Open clusters can contain anything from about a dozen to many hundreds of stars.

▲ The Lagoon Nebula is another large gas cloud in which stars are forming. A cluster of young stars can be seen embedded within the nebula. The light from these stars is causing the gas in the Lagoon Nebula to shine.

Globular Clusters

These are very large clusters which are ball- or globe-shaped. They contain thousands or even millions of stars. They are seen outside our Galaxy and move around the nucleus of the Galaxy in very long orbits.

◀ Tucanae is a globular cluster. This is a huge, globe-shaped collection of many thousands of stars.

Galaxies

Quasars

The most distant objects that we have seen are **quasars**. They are so far away that their light set off long before the Earth existed. Quasars lie almost at the edge of the Universe. Is there an end to the Universe? If not, then does space go on forever? One day, in the future, we may find out.

The Milky Way Galaxy

On a clear, dark night a faint, misty band of light may be seen stretching across the sky. This is the Milky Way, the combined light from thousands of faint stars. A closer look at the Milky Way through binoculars or a small telescope will show many of these stars.

Our Galaxy is shaped like a gigantic Catherine wheel with spiral arms coming out from a central bulge. The stars that form the Milky Way all lie in the Galaxy. Our Sun is roughly two thirds of the way out from the centre, near the edge of one of the spiral arms. We are unable to see right to the centre of the Galaxy because our view is blocked by dust that lies between the stars.

Clusters of Galaxies

Our Galaxy is a member of a cluster of galaxies. This cluster is known as the Local

This picture shows the Milky Way. It is the combined light from thousands of stars lying along the main plane of the Galaxy. The streak of light is the trail left by an artificial satellite. ▶

This picture shows a spiral galaxy similar to our own Milky Way Galaxy. However, we see this one looking edge-on. The dark band running across the galaxy is dust. This appears dark because it blocks out the light from the stars beyond. The bright centre, or nucleus, of the galaxy is visible. ▶

Group. There are more than twenty other galaxies in the Local Group. These include spiral, elliptical and irregular galaxies. Many other clusters of galaxies are known. Some of these contain only a few galaxies. Others are much larger. One of the largest is in the constellation of Perseus and has hundreds of members.

The Expanding Universe

Scientists do not know for sure how the Universe came into existence. We do know that the Universe came into being thousands of millions of years ago. This may have been because of a huge explosion which released matter into space. This explosion is known as the Big Bang. The matter from it formed galaxies, stars and planets. Some think that the Universe is still expanding from this tremendous explosion.

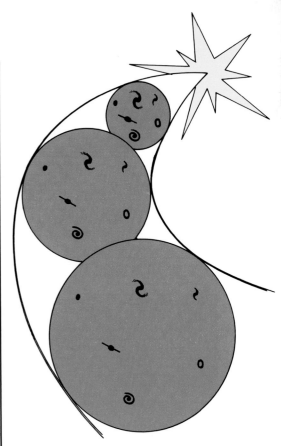

▲ **The Big Bang theory**: a huge explosion released matter into the universe.

▲ Galaxies are often classified by their shapes. Here are some of them.

◄ The Andromeda Galaxy is one of the nearest galaxies to us.

33

Finding the Pole Star

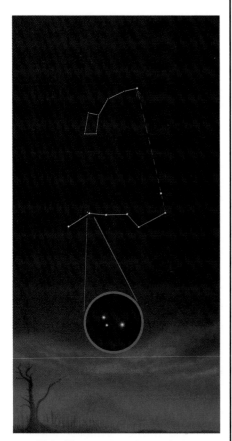

▲ This illustration shows how you can find the Pole Star using the pointers in Ursa Major (the Great Bear). The inset shows the double star – Alcor and Mizar.

Galileo was one of the first men to see the night sky through a telescope. ▶

Ursa Major (The Great Bear) is a large, sprawling constellation and most of its stars are quite faint. However, the seven brightest are arranged in a conspicuous pattern known as the Plough. A close look at the star in the middle of the Plough 'handle' will show that it is a double star. Binoculars will bring both stars out very well. These two stars are called Alcor and Mizar.

The two stars at the end of the Plough are often called the Pointers. If you follow an imaginary line from these you will come to the Pole Star. This is the brightest star in Ursa Minor (The Little Bear). We have already seen that the Earth's axis points towards the celestial poles. The Pole Star marks the position of the north celestial pole. If you face the Pole Star you are looking to the north. Finding the Plough is easy. During autumn evenings it can be seen low over the northern horizon. In winter it is high in the north-east. In spring it is almost overhead and in summer it can be seen in the north-west.

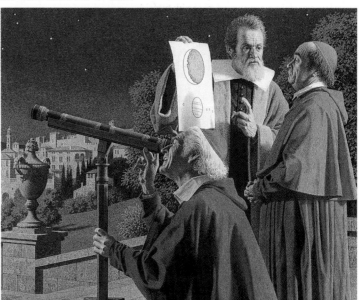

Spring

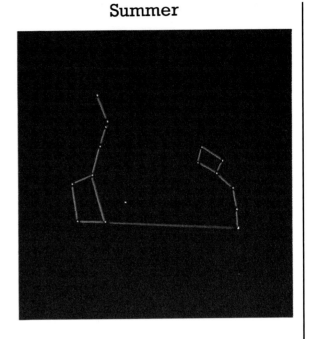

Summer

Ursa Major
(The Great Bear)

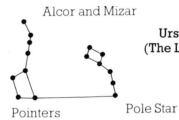

Alcor and Mizar

Pointers

Pole Star

Ursa Minor
(The Little Bear)

Autumn

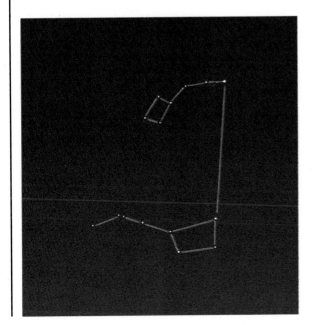

Winter

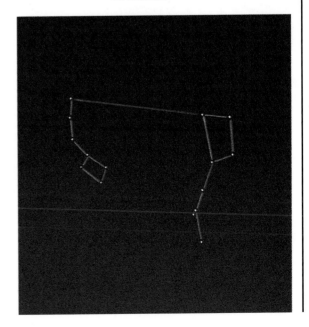

The Southern Cross

The Southern Cross: This constellation can only be seen from the Southern hemisphere. It is at its best in autumn. ▼

The Pole Star can only be seen from the northern hemisphere. It is never seen to rise from south of the equator. However, people in the southern hemisphere have their own constellations, some of which cannot be seen from the north. One of the most famous southern star groups is Crux (The Cross).

Crux is a small but prominent pattern of stars. It is also known as the Southern Cross. The constellation Centaurus (The Centaur) lies quite close to Crux. The two brightest stars in Centaurus are shown here. Alpha Centauri and Hadar are very bright. Together with Crux they make a very noticeable collection of stars. The best time of year to see the Southern Cross is during the autumn when it will be high up in the southern sky.

The Southern Cross

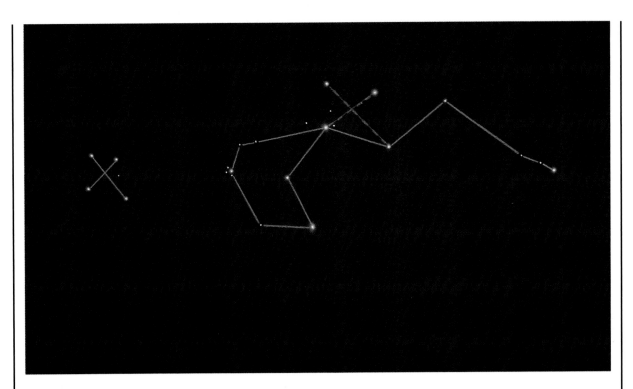

Carina

Carina was once part of a much larger constellation called Argo Navis. It represented the ship in which Jason and the Argonauts (people from Greek mythology) sailed in search of the Golden Fleece. Argo Navis was divided up into three smaller constellations. These are Vela (the Sails), Puppis (the **Poop**) and Carina (the **Keel**). Each of these is a part of the original ship.

Carina can be found very high in the south-western sky during autumn evenings in the southern hemisphere. Its brightest star is Canopus. This is a brilliant white star which is often used to help with spacecraft **navigation**. Canopus is the second brightest star in the entire sky.

Theta lies in the centre of a cluster of stars which is well worth a look through binoculars or a small telescope. Tureis lies at one of the points of a cross-shaped pattern of stars. Two of these stars lie in the constellation of Vela. This pattern is known as the "False Cross". It is often confused with Crux, the Southern Cross, which lies nearby.

▲ **Carina**: This constellation lies close to the Southern Cross (on the left). It was part of a constellation that the Greeks associated with Jason and the Argonauts, a figure out of their mythology.

Carina

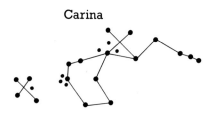

The Southern Cross

Hadar

Alpha Centauri

Stars and Myths

Many ancient people looked up at the stars and made patterns out of what they saw. They related the shapes to people, animals, gods and objects like boats or musical instruments. They named these patterns, or constellations, after them. Today we still use many of the names that the ancient Greeks gave to the stars. Here are just a few of these, which can be seen in the Northern or Southern Hemispheres.

Andromeda and Pegasus

For those in the northern hemisphere, Andromeda and Pegasus are the main autumn star groups. They can be seen high in the south during October and November evenings. Andromeda is the name of a beautiful maiden who was rescued from the sea monster by Perseus, an ancient Greek hero.

Andromeda contains the most distant object visible to the naked eye. This is the Andromeda Spiral Galaxy (see Galaxies page 32). To find it, first of all locate the line formed by the two stars Mu and Nu. The Andromeda Spiral Galaxy can be seen just to the right, or west, of Nu. It is visible to the naked eye as a faint, misty patch of light.

In the centre of this group of stars, you can see a square. This makes up the constellation Pegasus, the winged horse from Greek mythology. Also in this illustration is Andromeda, the beautiful maiden. She can be found below Pegasus, to the left. ▼

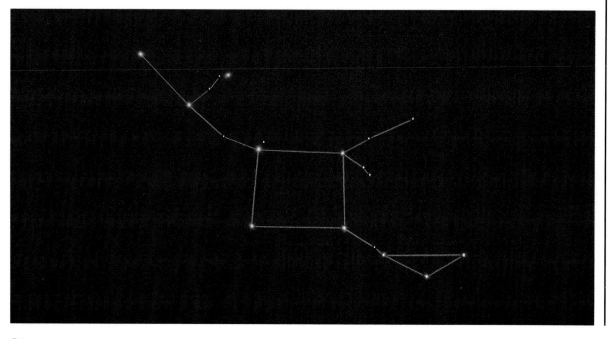

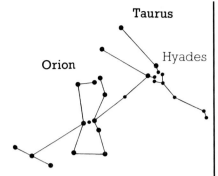

◄ Here you can see Orion in the centre of the picture. The imaginary line runs down to Sirius, the brightest star in the constellation of Canis Major (the Great Dog, see also page 6). It runs up to Aldebaron, a bright star in the constellation of Taurus (the Bull).

Pegasus is named after the legendary winged horse of Greek mythology. The four main stars in this group form the Square of Pegasus. When seen on star maps, the Square looks quite bright. However, most of the stars making up the Square are fairly faint. At first, you may have difficulty finding it. Once you have seen it, you will easily find it again.

One of the stars in the Square is Alpheratz. This is actually a member of Andromeda and is only "borrowed" to complete the Square. Scheat has an orange-red tint. This can be seen with the naked eye if the sky is really dark and clear. A pair of binoculars will show that Enif is also orange.

From north of the equator, look for Orion high in the south during winter evenings. From south of the equator, Orion can be seen high in the north during summer. The Belt of Orion acts as a 'pointer' to the star Sirius. This is the brightest star in Canis Major (The Great Dog). It also points the other way to Aldebaran. This is the brightest star in Taurus (The Bull). Two star clusters can be seen. These are the Hyades (HI'-ADES) and the Pleiades (PLY'-ADES). This chart shows how these star groups appear from the north.

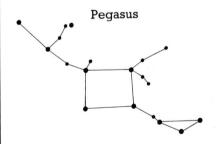

6: EXPLORATION

Into Space and Back

▲ The first manned landing on the Moon was made by astronauts on the Apollo 11 mission in July 1969. There were three astronauts on board: Neil Armstrong, Edwin Aldrin and Michael Collins. These pictures show the launch of Apollo 11. ▶

The Countdown

When a spacecraft launch is shown on television, it usually goes from ten down to one and lift-off! However, the complete countdown sequence is much longer than this. Exactly how long depends upon how complicated the mission is. During the countdown,

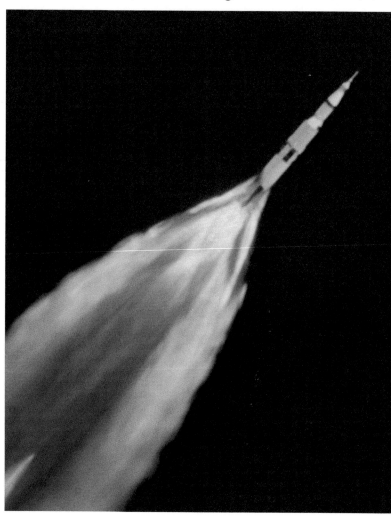

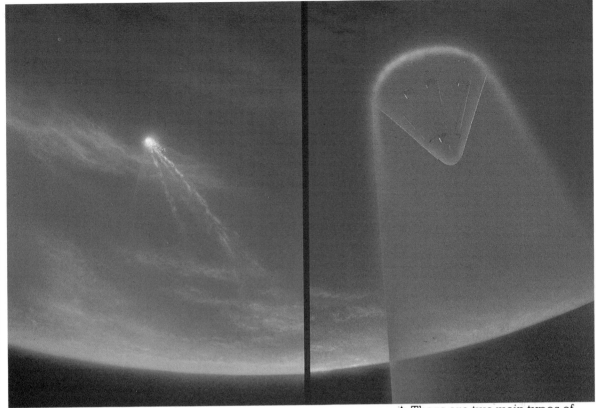

▲ There are two main types of re-entry into Earth: one in which the satellite burns up and one in which the craft is returned safely.

computers continually check the spacecraft, systems are started and the general health of the craft and crew are followed. During the final seconds, engines are started just before lift-off. Countdown can be held up at any time if there are problems.

Into Orbit
The spacecraft is guided more or less **automatically** during its climb into orbit. Computers control the flight path. A flight speed high enough to overcome the pull of Earth's gravity must be reached before the spacecraft can get into orbit.

Re-entry and Return to Earth
Many unmanned satellites eventually undergo orbital decay. This means that the orbital height gets less, eventually causing the satellite to enter the upper atmosphere. It then falls out of orbit and down to the surface, burning up on the way.

Different Orbits

The type of orbit that a spacecraft uses depends upon its mission. Some satellites travel around the Earth once every twenty-four hours in the same direction that the Earth is rotating. This means that they remain above the same point on the surface. Communication and television satellites use this type of orbit. Satellites which look at the entire surface of the Earth, such as weather satellites, travel in a different orbit. They orbit the Earth in paths which take them alternately over the north and south poles. Because the Earth is rotating below, the satellite will pass over a different region during each orbit.

Unmanned Space Flights

A view of Earth from space. ▶ You can see the swirling masses of cloud moving over land and sea. Weather satellites follow the movement of this cloud.

The first artificial satellite was launched by the Russians on 4th October 1957. It was called Sputnik 1. It carried radio equipment which was used to send signals back to the scientists on Earth. ▼

With manned flights, re-entry is controlled. Rockets bring the vehicle down into the atmosphere. In order to protect the craft and crew, special heat shields are built on to the spacecraft to absorb the heat generated during re-entry. In the case of the Space Shuttle, protective tiles are fastened to the Orbiter (see pages 50-51). Generally, spacecraft make the final descent by parachute, although the Shuttle glides down to the surface rather like a huge, unpowered aircraft.

Unmanned Satellites

The first satellite was Sputnik 1. This was launched by the Russians in 1957. This marked the beginning of the Space Age. Since then many more satellites have been launched. They are used for many different purposes including weather forecasting, communications and Earth-observation. Some satellites are used for military purposes, although these are usually kept very secret. Today many different countries have their own satellites and there is now a great number in orbit around the Earth.

▲ Astronomers use satellites to carry out observations from space. This is so that they can examine the sky without having to peer through the atmosphere. This picture shows a special satellite that was used to look at ultraviolet energy from the stars.

Different Types of Satellite

Satellites play an important part in weather forecasting. From high above the Earth they take photographs of wide areas of our planet. These pictures tell us a great deal about cloud movement, winds and so on. Violent storms and hurricanes can also be detected. Early warnings can then be given and many lives have been saved in this way.

Earth-observation satellites carry out many different tasks. Some are used to help scientists find valuable minerals below the Earth's surface. Satellites also help us to control pollution. From orbit a satellite can see such things as oil slicks, forest fires and even crop diseases. Many of these are difficult to pinpoint from Earth until they become out of hand.

Astronomy from Space

Satellites are used by astronomers to help them observe stars and other objects in the sky. Special instruments are carried high above the atmosphere. Here they carry out observations that are difficult or impossible to do from the ground.

Space Telescopes

A rather unusual "satellite" will be the Space Telescope, which is due to be launched in December 1989 on the Space Shuttle. This is a large optical telescope which will help astronomers study the sky from well above the atmosphere. They will be able to see objects fifty times fainter and seven times further away than they can now. They will also be able to see much further into space than ever before. The Space Telescope will give us a better understanding of the Universe in which we live.

Spacesuits

▲ A Shuttle astronaut is seen here wearing the Manned Manoeuvring Unit. This special backpack allows the astronaut to move in any direction.

What is a Spacesuit?

A spacesuit is special clothing designed to protect an astronaut from the dangers of space. These include very large changes in temperature, harmful **radiation** from the Sun, fast-moving particles of space dust and the **vacuum** of space where there is no oxygen. A spacesuit has many layers, each of which has a special purpose. One of the inner layers controls the temperature inside the suit. This is done by passing water through plastic tubing that is threaded through it. This runs hot or cold depending on the outside temperature.

It takes many months to make a spacesuit. Each part must be tested thoroughly after which they are assembled and tested again. This is to make sure that the spacesuit will stand up to the wear and tear it will get on a space mission.

In the early years of space exploration, each astronaut had a suit especially made. Now, each suit is made up from a number of different pieces. Each of these pieces is made in a selection of sizes. Each astronaut can be given a suit to fit from these.

On the back of the suit is a backpack. This is known as the Primary Life-Support System (PLSS). It holds enough water and oxygen to enable the astronaut to carry out space walks of several hours. On Earth, the backpack weighs around 115 kg (250 lbs); in the weightless conditions of space it weighs nothing.

The Manned Manoeuvring Unit

The Manned Manoeuvring Unit (MMU) is a special backpack. It allows the astronaut to leave the spacecraft and fly independently from it. It has two gas tanks which supply gas to thruster jets. The astronaut uses special controls on the MMU to release gas from these jets. This enables the astronaut to steer through space in any direction. The MMU is very heavy and on Earth weighs almost 158 kgs (350 lbs). However, when used in space it makes the astronaut very mobile.

Spacesuit and Manned Manoeuvring Unit

Hard upper torso

Communications carrier assembly
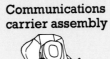

Arm assembly
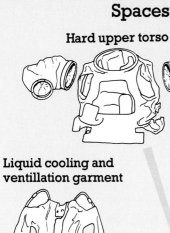

Liquid cooling and ventillation garment

Display and control module

Airlock adapter plate

Helmet and visor assembly

Primary life support subsystem

Electrical harness

Gloves

Secondary oxygen pack

Lower torso assembly

Insuit drink bag

Service and cooling umbilical

Urine collection device

Contamination control cartridge

Battery

Early Manned Spaceflights

▲ The first woman in space was the Russian, Valentina Tereshkova. She orbited the Earth 48 times in Vostok 6 in June 1963.

The Russian cosmonaut, Yuri Gagarin, was the first man to go into space. He orbited the Earth once in Vostok 1 in April 1961. ▶

The first man in space was the Russian cosmonaut, Yuri Gagarin. His spacecraft was called Vostock 1 and was launched in April, 1961. It was known before the flight that Gagarin would be weightless when in space. It was thought by some that this might be harmful to him. However, all went well during the mission. Gargarin made one orbit of the Earth which was followed by a safe landing.

The Next Steps into Space

The next two space flights were both made by American astronauts. The first of these was Alan Shepard. He flew to a height of just over 160 kms (100 miles) before splashing down in the Atlantic Ocean. This was followed with a flight by Virgil Grissom. So far, however, the Americans had not put a man into orbit around the Earth. Before they did, the Russian cosmonaut Gherman Titov spent over a day orbiting the Earth.

During the mission, Titov suffered from space sickness. This is similar to ordinary travel sickness. It is due to weightlessness affecting the balancing mechanism inside the ears. Titov did recover during the flight. Space sickness is one of the more unpleasant side-effects of space flight.

A few months after Titov's flight, John Glenn became the first American astronaut to actually orbit the Earth. Like Shepard and Grissom

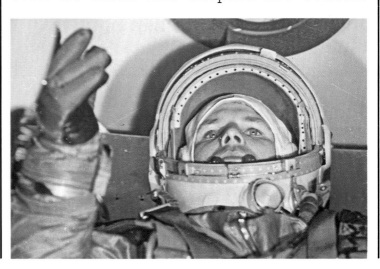

The Russians launched the first three-man crew on board Voskhod 1 in October, 1964. This was a very dangerous mission. The spacecraft was a Vostok craft. Like the American Mercury capsules, it was designed to carry one man only. It had to be modified to carry another two. The three cosmonauts had to travel without their bulky spacesuits to give them enough room. The flight was successful and the crew returned safely back to Earth. Voskhod 2 followed almost half a year later. This was the first two-man flight. One of the crew was Alexei Leonov. He carried out the first ever space walk during this mission.

◄ In June 1965 Ed White became the first American to walk in space. This was during the Gemini 4 mission. White used a hand-held jet gun to propel himself around in space.

These are early manned spacecraft. ▼

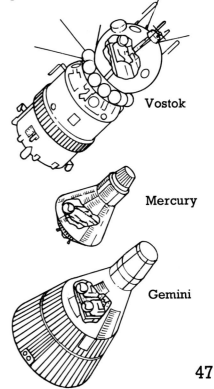

Vostok

Mercury

Gemini

before him, he flew inside one of the Mercury **capsules**. Glenn's flight lasted almost five hours after which he splashed down safely.

The Gemini Programme

The American Gemini craft were designed to carry two men into space. The Gemini craft were capable of changing their orbits, and meeting and joining with other craft. American astronauts began to make much longer spaceflights and carried out a number of space walks. The first American space walk was made by Ed White on the Gemini 4 flight. The steps taken during these flights helped pave the way for the Apollo missions.

The Moon Landings

Disaster Strikes!

Disaster struck on the Apollo 13 flight. On the way to the Moon there was an explosion in the Service Module. An oxygen tank had been destroyed, causing damage. There was a loss of electrical power and the lives of the crew were in danger. It was decided that they should transfer to the Lunar Module and use it as a lifeboat to see them home. The spacecraft eventually went round the Moon and set course back to Earth. Saving power where they could they survived the journey home, although condtions were very uncomfortable. Happily, to the relief of the waiting world, Apollo 13 splashed down safely. Apollo 13 had shown that space was a dangerous place.

This view shows the Lunar Rover and Lunar Module on the Moon's surface during the Apollo 15 mission. The tracks left by the Rover can be seen in the lunar soil, as can the footprints of the astronauts. In the background we can see lunar mountains. ▶

The Early Flights

Apollo 7 flew in October, 1968. It was the first Apollo flight with people on board. During this mission the astronauts carried out tests on the Command and Service Modules. Apollo 8 took men to the Moon and back for the first time. The astronauts only flew around the Moon and did not actually land. They took pictures of the far side. Apollo 9 was similar to Apollo 7. This time, though, the Lunar Module was taken into Earth orbit. The flight lasted 10 days.

There was one more flight before the Moon-landings. This was the Apollo 10 mission. Here, the complete Apollo craft was flown to the Moon. The Lunar Module separated from the Command Module while in orbit around the Moon. It was then taken down to within a few kilometres of the Moon's surface.

Walking on the Moon

The Apollo 11 mission took place in July, 1969. The three astronauts were Neil Armstrong, Edwin Aldrin and Michael Collins. The lift-off went well and three days later the spacecraft reached the Moon and went into orbit around it. After twelve orbits the Lunar Module separated. It started its descent to the lunar surface with Armstrong and Aldrin on board. The Lunar Module touched down in the *Mare Tranquillitatis*. Neil Armstrong climbed down the ladder on the side of the Lunar Module, and became the first person to step on to the surface of the Moon. Aldrin followed Armstrong a short time later. The two astronauts stayed on the lunar surface for over two hours. They collected rock and soil samples and left experiments there. The upper part of the Lunar Module took them back up to the waiting Collins. The crew then returned to Earth.

▲ American astronaut Edwin Aldrin stands on the lunar surface next to the American flag. This was during the Apollo 11 mission in July 1969. The footprints of the astronauts can be seen in the lunar soil. The Lunar Module can be seen at right.

The Lunar Rover

The last four flights went smoothly. On the final three missions the astronauts took with them the Lunar Rover. This was a kind of "Moon-car" which was carried in the base of the Lunar Module. It enabled the astronauts to explore wide areas of the lunar surface. During the three missions the Lunar Rover carried them almost 100 km (60 miles) across the Moon's surface.

The Space Shuttle

Here we see the Space Shuttle above the Earth. Two astronauts are moving out to collect a satellite which needs repairing in the Shuttle cargo bay. A special robot arm is used to help them retrieve the satellite from orbit. ▶

What is the Space Shuttle?

The Space Shuttle is a re-usable spacecraft. It is launched into space like a rocket and returns from space like a huge glider. Normally, the rockets that are used to launch astronauts and satellites into space are thrown away. However, the Space Shuttle can be used many times. This has greatly reduced the cost of spaceflight.

Uses of the Shuttle

The Space Shuttle can be used for many different things. It can carry satellites into orbit and even bring satellites back to Earth for repair. Satellites have also been serviced and repaired while still in orbit.

Satellites or other scientific equipment are carried in a special compartment. This is the payload bay. Once the Shuttle is in orbit, two large doors which cover the payload bay are opened, exposing it to space. This also helps to keep the spacecraft cool.

Launch and Return to Earth

The main part of the space Shuttle is the Orbiter. This is the section which contains the flight deck, living quarters and payload bay.

A Shuttle flight is controlled by the Commander and a pilot astronaut. They are helped both by computers on board the Shuttle and by a team back on Earth. During each flight, the people on board the Shuttle do not wear spacesuits. The atmosphere inside the spacecraft is carefully controlled. It is similar to the atmosphere on the Earth. The only time that spacesuits are worn is when astronauts venture outside the Orbiter.

At the time of launch, a large fuel tank and two extra boosters are attached to the Orbiter. The fuel tank supplies fuel to the main engines at the rear of the Orbiter. Extra power is provided by the two boosters. Around two minutes into the flight, the boosters are ejected.

The Shuttle Orbiter has a pair of smaller engines. These are fired to lift the spacecraft into its orbit. They are used again at the end of the mission to bring the Orbiter back down into the atmosphere. Other spacecraft have special heat shields to prevent them from burning up during re-entry. The outer surface of the Orbiter is covered with protective, heat-resistant tiles and blankets. These can easily be replaced between missions. The Orbiter glides down through the atmosphere. It lands rather like an aircraft on a long runway.

This is the Shuttle taking off. It carries a large fuel tank and two extra boosters to give it the power needed to launch itself. The boosters are ejected after about 2 minutes. ▼

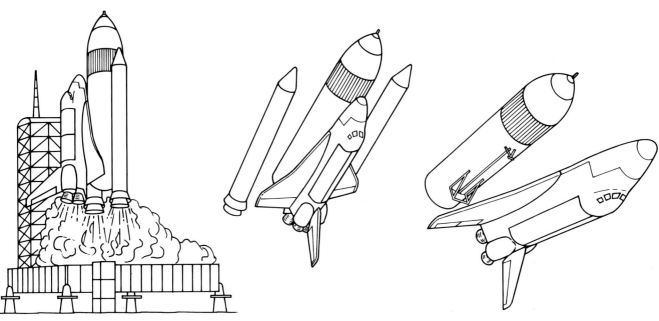

Shuttle launch   **Ejecting boosters**   **Ejecting the fuel tank**   51

7: THE FUTURE

Probes to the Planets

Before the Space Age, astronomers could only look at the Moon and planets through telescopes here on Earth. The planets lie at large distances. Because of this we could not learn all we wanted to know about these worlds. This all changed when astronomers were able to send space probes to other planets.

Missions to the Moon
The first world to be explored this way was the Moon. The first pictures of the Moon's far side were taken in 1959. These were from the Russian Luna 3 spacecraft. Since then, many other space probes have been sent to the Moon. Some of these have actually landed on the surface and sent back pictures to Earth. Samples of lunar soil have even been brought back for scientists to study.

Exploring the Planets
Many of the planets have been visted by space probes. The only mission to Mercury, the

Voyager
A number of probes have been sent to explore the outer planets. The most outstanding of these are the American Voyager craft. Voyager 1 has told us a great deal about both Jupiter and Saturn. Voyager 2 has gone even further. As well as flying past Jupiter and Saturn it has visited Uranus. It is due to reach Neptune in August 1989. This will then become the most distant planet to be explored by space probe.

This is Pioneer passing Venus. ▶

innermost planet, was the American Mariner 10 craft. This flew past the planet three times in 1974 and 1975. It sent back thousands of photographs of Mercury's surface. There have been many flights to Venus. Venus is covered in dense clouds. Because of this, space probes that have either flown past or gone into orbit around the planet could not photograph the surface. Some probes have penetrated the clouds and landed on the surface of Venus, while others have mapped the surface using special radar techniques. Because the surface conditions are so hostile (see pages 18-21) these probes must be specially designed to operate there. The first mission to produce photographs of the surface was that of the Russian Venera 9 craft. This landed on Venus in 1975. This was the first time that pictures have been received from the surface of another planet.

Eventually, spacecraft will be sent to all the planets in the Solar System. Many of the minor planets will also be explored this way. Comets will be examined with space probes, as happened with Halley's Comet in 1986.

▲ This photograph was taken by Viking 1, one of two American spacecraft that landed on Mars in 1976. Part of the Viking 1 spacecraft can be seen in the corner of the picture.

Looking at Mars

The first successful mission to Mars was by the American Mariner 4 craft. This flew past Mars in 1965 and sent back over twenty pictures of the Martian terrain. Two spacecraft have actually landed on the surface of Mars and sent back photographs and other information. These were the American Viking 1 and Viking 2 craft.

Space Stations

A space station is a place where astronauts and scientists live and work. It goes round the Earth in an **orbit**. Scientists can carry out experiments impossible to do on Earth because of **gravity**. There is no gravity in space. These experiments may include medical research and studying the planets and stars. Space stations get their power from solar panels which turn sunlight into electricity.

Salyut and Skylab

The first space station was the Soviet Salyut 1. It was launched in 1971. Altogether there were seven Salyuts. They were all specially built to carry out experiments in space.

The American Skylab was launched in 1973. It was built out of part of the Saturn V rocket. There were a total of three Skylab crews. Their mission in space ended in 1974.

This is Skylab going round the ▲ Earth at a height of over 400 km (250 miles). During its launch, one of the solar panels at the front fell off. The other failed to open. The first crew had to free it.

This is a scientist's idea of the ▶ Space Shuttle docking onto a space station. It was designed by NASA (National Aeronautics and Space Administration) in America.

The latest Soviet space station is called Mir. It will form the centre on to which four modules can be docked. It will be used for studying the universe, carrying out biological experiments and medical research. Unmanned craft can also link up with Mir. These will supply provisions for the crew.

The Soviet Mir space station. ▲ It was completed in 1986.

Living in Space

A large space station is also being planned by the Americans. The parts for it will be made on Earth. These will be taken into space and put together. The station will have a number of uses, including repairing **satellites** and building smaller space vehicles.

Soon people will be able to live in space for as long as they want. Space stations now being built will be permanently lived in.

Colonies on other Planets

One day, observatories may be built on the Moon. This will give astronomers a great advantage when looking at distant stars, because there is no atmosphere on the Moon.

▼

Lunar Bases

The first space colonies will be in orbit around the Earth. Eventually, other colonies will be built either orbiting other planets or on their surfaces. The first of these may be on the Moon. This could be by the early part of the twenty-first century. The Moon is rich in raw materials including iron and bauxite. These could be mined and used for building other colonies. Farms could be set up and the lunar soil used to grow crops. There could also be workshops and laboratories.

Colonies on Other Planets

Most of the other planets in the Solar System are unsuitable for manned bases. Mercury and Venus are too hot. Jupiter, Saturn, Uranus and Neptune are all gaseous planets and do not have solid surfaces. However, colonies may be built on some of the asteroids. These would be used to mine the raw materials that are

there. Colonies could also be built on the satellites of some of the other planets.

Mars will probably be the first planet to be colonized. Astronauts will visit the planet. These will be followed by the first colonists who will set up permanent bases. These would have living quarters, farms and working areas. Mines would extract the raw materials from under the Martian surface. These colonies, like those on the Moon, would be entirely self-supporting.

Travel to the Stars

One day people may travel out to the stars. This will be a long time in the future. The stars all lie at great distances. The rockets we have today would take thousands of years to get to even the nearest stars. New and faster spaceships will be needed, and nuclear powered rockets may help us. Even then a journey to the stars will take many years.

▲ These people are taking samples of rock from the surrounding landscape to take back to the colony to analyse.

People living in colonies for long periods of time will need to be able to feed themselves. ▼

Alien Life

The Search for Alien Life

There are thousands of millions of stars in our Galaxy and thousands of millions of other galaxies. It is widely believed that intelligent life may exist on planets going round other

◀ There is no reason to suppose that intelligent aliens will look much different to humans. Here we see an inhabitant of another world which, unlike earth, has two moons and a brilliant white star shining in its sky.

The Pioneer 10 and Pioneer 11 spacecraft are now on their way out of the Solar System. Each one carries a plaque with a message from its human builders. This contains a picture of the Pioneer craft and two humans drawn to the same scale. ▼

◀◀ Will colonies on other planets make contact with alien life?

stars. Scientists and astronomers are trying to make contact with them. This is being done in a number of different ways. American scientists have put messages from Earth onto four spacecraft. These were launched to explore the outer planets. Eventually they will leave the Solar System. They may be found in interstellar space by an **alien** civilization. However, the chances of this happening are very small in comparision to the vastness of space.

What Would aliens Look Like?

If we did find other creatures in the Galaxy, what would they be like? This would depend on what conditions were like on their home planet. Cold worlds may have beings with fur-covered bodies. This would be a protection against the low temperatures. Hot planets may be home to creatures with special skin to protect them against the heat. Planets with dim suns would be darker. This might produce creatures with large eyes. These would help them to see in the semi-darkness. The list of possibilities is endless. One thing is for certain. Whatever they do look like, it will be different to we humans here on Earth. We can only guess how different until we make contact and see for ourselves.

Glossary

Alien: A being or creature who comes from elsewhere, such as another country, or another planet.

Asteroid: One of a number of small planet-like objects, most of which orbit the Sun between Mars and Jupiter.

Astronomer: A person who studies the sky and the objects in it.

Atmosphere: Layer of gas surrounding a planet.

Atoms: Tiny particles from which all substances are made.

Automatic: Work carried out by a machine or other equipment, such as a robot.

Axis: A line through an object around which it spins, like the handle of a spinning top.

Calendar: The division of the year into days and months.

Capsule: In space flight, the part of a spacecraft in which people travel into space.

Colonize: To travel to and settle in a place. Early settlers colonized America. In future, people from Earth may colonize space and the planets.

Comet: Clumps of ice, gas and dust orbiting the Sun. When they get close to the Sun, the Sun's heat makes the comet throw off gas and dust which form the comet's tail.

Constellation: A pattern of stars in the sky. There are a total of 88 constellations.

Ellipse: A shape similar to an oval. The orbits of planets round the Sun are elliptical.

Equator: An imaginary line running around the Earth (or other astronomical object) midway between the North and South Poles.

Galaxies: Gigantic collections of stars, many of which also contain gas and dust. Galaxies can be any of a number of different shapes. Our own Galaxy, of which the Sun is a member, is shaped like a huge Catherine Wheel.

Gas: A substance, like air or steam, which is not solid or liquid.

Gravity: The force which holds objects to the Earth, or to any other astronomical object. Gravity keeps the planets in orbit around the Sun.

Helium: A gas and the second most common substance in the Universe.

Hydrogen: A colourless gas and the most common substance in the Universe.

Keel: The lower part of a ship. The constellation Carina (the Keel) was once part of the much larger constellation Argo Navis, the Ship Argo. This was the ship in which Jason sailed to find the Golden Fleece.

Lava: Molten matter thrown out of volcanoes which goes solid when it cools down.

Light year: The unit of length used by astronomers to express distances to stars and other objects. The distance light travels in a year: it is equal to over 9 million million kilometres!

Magnification: Increase in the apparent size of an object. Astronomers use telescopes to magnify planets, galaxies and other objects in the sky.

Magnitude: The system astronomers use to describe the brightness of stars or other objects in the sky.

Meteor: The streak of light in the sky created by a tiny particle which has entered the Earth's atmosphere and which burns up.

Meteorite: A particle which enters the atmosphere and which is large enough to survive the fall to Earth.

Milky Way: The faint band of light seen crossing the sky. It is made up from the glow of thousands of stars which lie along the main plane of our Galaxy.

Navigation: Directing the course of a ship or other craft.

Observatory: A building, usually housing a telescope, from where astronomers study the sky.

Orbit: The path of an object as it travels around another. For example, the orbit of the Earth around the Sun.

Phase: In astronomy, the apparent shape of the Moon or a planet as seen from Earth. For example, a crescent Moon or a full Moon.

Planet: One of the nine main members of the Sun's family.

Poop: The stern, or rear part, of a ship. The constellation Puppis, the Poop or Stern, was once part of the constellation Argo Navis.

Prominences: Huge masses of glowing gas, mainly hydrogen, which rise from the surface of the Sun.

Quasars: Very distant and very luminous objects, now known to be at the centres of very energetic galaxies.

Radiation: Energy given out by objects. Light and heat are both types of radiation. So are X-rays, gamma rays and radio waves. Stars and other objects in the sky give out many different kinds of radiation.

Radio telescope: A special type of telescope designed to pick up radio waves from stars and other objects in the sky.

Radio wave: See **Radiation**.

Red giant: A large star which is very bright.

Reflector: The type of telescope which uses a specially shaped mirror to collect starlight.

Refractor: The type of telescope which uses.a lens to collect starlight.

Satellite: A small object orbiting a larger one. For example, artificial satellites orbit the Earth and many of the planets have moons, or satellites, in orbit around them.

Solar system: The system of planets, asteroids, comets and other objects orbiting the Sun.

Space probe: A spacecraft sent by scientists and astronomers to examine planets and other objects from close range.

Stars: Hot, luminous balls of gas which appear as twinkling points of light in the sky.

Supernova: A colossal explosion which marks the death of a very massive star.

Telescope: A device used by astronomers for looking at stars and other objects in the sky.

Vacuum: An area which contains no matter of any kind.

White dwarf: A small, very dense star, which is nearing the end of its life.

Year: The time it takes for the Earth, or other planets, to orbit the Sun. An Earth year is $365\frac{1}{4}$ days long, while a year on Pluto lasts 248 Earth years! This is how long it takes for Pluto to travel around the Sun! See **Calendar**.

Index

64